women's lip

Outrageous, Irreverent and Just Plain Hilarious Quotes

edited by Roz Warren

SOURCEBOOKS HYSTERIA™
AN IMPRINT OF SOURCEBOOKS, INC.®
NAPERVILLE, ILLINOIS

Published by Sourcebooks, Inc.
P.O. Box 4410
Naperville, IL 60567-4410
630-961-3900
Fax: 630-961-2168
www.sourcebooks.com

ISBN 1-4022-0391-8

Printed and bound in Canada.
WC 10 9 8 7 6 5 4 3 2 1

This book is dedicated with love
to my son Thomas.

"Wit happens."

—*Karyn Buxman*

—Age—

I'd like to grow very old
as slowly as possible.
—*Irene Meyer Selznick*

The hardest years in life are those
between ten and seventy.
—*Helen Hayes (at 73)*

My mother used to say:
the older you get, the better you get—
unless you're a banana.

—*Rose,* The Golden Girls

The secret of staying young is to live
honestly, eat slowly,
and lie about your age.

—*Lucille Ball*

No animal should ever jump up on the dining-room furniture unless absolutely certain that he can hold his own in the conversation.

—Fran Lebowitz

—ART—

Art is spirituality in drag.
—*Jennifer Unlimited*

If you have a burning, restless urge
to write or paint, simply eat something sweet
and the feeling will pass.
—*Fran Lebowitz*

—BANKS—

My Aunt Eula's bank in Fort Worth has been
swallowed so many times by bigger banks,
she calls it "Edible National."

—Molly Ivins

I bank at a woman's bank. It's closed
three or four days a month due to cramps.

—Judy Carter

—BREAKING UP—

Book title:
Get Your Tongue Out Of My Mouth,
I'm Kissing You Goodbye
—*Cynthia Heimel*

If you love someone, set them free.
If they come back,
they're probably broke.
—*Rhonda Dicksion*

I broke up
with my boyfriend because
he wanted
to get married.
I didn't want him to.

—Rita Rudner

Q: What do you do when
your boyfriend walks out?
A: Shut the door.

—*Angela Martin*

Some people have their marriages annulled,
which means they never existed.
Boy, talk about denial! What do you say when
people see your wedding album?
"Oh that was just some play I was in."

—*Carol Leifer*

—BREASTS—

A lot of guys think the larger a woman's breasts are,
the less intelligent she is. I don't think it
works like that. I think it's the opposite.
I think the larger a woman's breasts are,
the less intelligent the men become.

—*Anita Wise*

Who ever thought up the word "Mammogram?"
Every time I hear it, I think I'm supposed to put
my breast in an envelope and send it to someone.

—*Jan King*

—Cars—

A car is just a moving, giant handbag!
You never have to actually carry groceries,
or dry cleaning, or anything! You can have
five pairs of shoes with you at all times!

—Cynthia Heimel

If you live in Beverly Hills
they don't put blinkers in your car.
They figure if you're that rich you don't have
to tell people where you're going.

—Bette Midler

—CATS—

Even my cat's depressed lately— I had the exterminators in and they killed all his toys.

—Anita Wise

Cats think about three things:
food, sex, and nothing.

—*Adair Lara*

I wonder what goes through his mind
when he sees us peeing in his water bowl.

—*Penny Ward Moser*

I found out why cats drink out of the toilet.
My mother told me it's because
it's cold in there. And I'm like:
"How did my mother know that?"
—*Wendy Liebman*

Dogs come when they're called.
Cats take a message and get back to you.
—*Mary Bly*

By and large, people who enjoy teaching animals to roll over will find themselves happier with a dog.

—*Barbara Holland*

Your cat will never threaten your popularity by barking at three in the morning. He won't attack the mailman or eat the drapes, although he may climb the drapes to see how the room looks from the ceiling.

—*Helen Powers*

I'm used to dogs.
When you leave them in the morning,
they stick their nose in the door crack
and stand there like a portrait
until you turn the key eight hours later.
A cat would never put up with that kind
of rejection. When you returned,
she'd stalk you until you dozed off
and then suck the air out of your body.

—Erma Bombeck

Kittens have different nutritional needs than adult cats. Consult with your veterinarian and then, for the good of your relationship with your cat, forget everything she tells you.

—*Nicole Hollander*

When my cats aren't happy, I'm not happy. Not because I care about their mood but because I know they're just sitting there thinking up ways to get even.

—*Penny Ward Moser*

—CELEBRITY—

I was the toast of two continents:
Greenland and Australia.

—*Dorothy Parker*

I never made Who's Who but
I'm featured in What's That.

—*Phyllis Diller*

I stopped believing in Santa Claus
at an early age. Mother took me in to see
him in a department store and
he asked me for my autograph.

—*Shirley Temple Black*

On Camille Paglia: The "g" is silent—
the only thing about her that is.

—*Julie Burchill*

What would happen if Mozart were alive today? After composing his first symphony at the age of four he would be Time's Man of the Year. He and his family would move to the Malibu Colony.

He'd host "Saturday Night Live."

He'd sign with Michael Ovitz, who'd package a sitcom for him. It would fail, as all sitcoms do, and little Mozart would go on drinking sprees and end up in rehab. At the age of, say, seven, Mozart would be a regular on "Hollywood Squares."

—Cynthia Heimel

I'm not offended by all the dumb-blonde jokes because I know that I'm not dumb. I also know I'm not blonde.

—*Dolly Parton*

—CELIBACY—

No sex is better than bad sex.

—*Germaine Greer*

I've reached that point in life
where you have to choose between happiness
and getting laid. I'm happy.
—*Mary Frances Connelly*

It's been so long since I made love,
I can't even remember who gets tied up.
—*Joan Rivers*

If they can put a man on the moon
why can't they put one in me?
—*Flash Rosenberg*

To me, "sexual freedom" means freedom
from having to have sex.
—*Lily Tomlin*

—CHILDBIRTH—

Dr. Simpson's first patient,
a doctor's wife in 1847,
had been so carried away with
enthusiasm that she christened
her child, a girl, "Anesthesia."

—*Elizabeth Longford*

I realize why women die in childbirth—
it's preferable.

—*Sherry Glaser*

The biggest drawback with the birth center
is that they make you dispose of
your own placenta. They discuss it with you
beforehand, so we debated with our friends what we
should do with it. One person
suggested we drive to the nearest Roy Rogers and
throw it in the dumpster.

—*Cathy Crimmins*

—Children—

A man finds out what is meant
by spitting image when
he tries to feed cereal to his infant.

—*Imogene Fey*

Never allow your child
to call you by your first name.
He hasn't known you long enough.

—*Fran Lebowitz*

Kids are like husbands—
they're fine as long as they're
someone else's.

—*Marsha Warfield*

I met this guy who said he loved children,
then I found out
he was on parole for it.

—*Monica Piper*

Last night I was at this dinner party and my girlfriend pointed this guy out to me and said, "Check him out—he just got divorced. He's available." As soon as dinner was over, this guy walked over to me. He didn't know my name. He didn't know anything about me. But he said he'd been watching me and that he loved me. And that he wanted me to have his child. And he gave me his child.

—Karen Haber

My mom used to say
it doesn't matter how many kids you have...
because one kid'll take up 100% of your time
so more kids can't possibly take up
more than 100% of your time.

—*Karen Brown*

Boys will be noise.

—*Nina Malkin*

Children ask better questions than adults.
"May I have a cookie?" "Why is the sky blue?"
and "What does a cow say?" are far more
likely to elicit a cheerful response than
"Where's your manuscript?" "Why haven't
you called?" and "Who's your lawyer?"

—*Fran Lebowitz*

I want to have children while my parents are
still young enough to take care of them.

—*Rita Rudner*

Ask your child what he wants for dinner
only if he's buying.

—*Fran Lebowitz*

Little girls are cute and small only to adults.
To one another they are not cute.
They are life-sized.

—*Margaret Atwood*

*I have to admit
I like Christmas cards—
even though they are
technically only junk mail
from people you know.*

—Patricia Marx

—COFFEE—

I believe humans get a lot done,
not because we're smart, but because
we have thumbs so we can make coffee.

—*Flash Rosenberg*

The only thing better than Great Sex...
is Great Coffee!

—*Stephanie Piro*

Never drink black coffee at lunch.
It will keep you awake in the afternoon.

—*Jilly Cooper*

Behind every successful woman…
is a substantial amount of coffee.

—*Stephanie Piro*

—COMMUNICATION—

The only thing I ever said to my parents when
I was a teenager was "Hang up, I got it!"

—Carol Leifer

—COMPLAINTS—

I personally believe we developed language
because of our deep inner need to complain.

—Jane Wagner

I have a "carpe diem" mug
and, truthfully,
at six in the morning
the words do not make me
want to seize the day.
They make me want
to slap a dead poet.

—Joanne Sherman

—CONTRACEPTION—

For a single woman, the most effective method of oral contraception is to just yell out, "Yes, yes, I want to have your baby!!"
—*Marsha Doble*

I'm Catholic. My mother and I were unpacking and she found my diaphragm. I had to tell her it was a bathing cap for my cat.
—*Lizz Winstead*

I was on stage last night and I said,
"You know the diaphragm
is a pain in the ass." Someone yelled out,
"You're putting it in the wrong place."
—*Carole Montgomery*

A friend of mine confused her valium with
her birth control pills—she had 14 kids
but she didn't give a shit.
—*Joan Rivers*

—COSMETIC SURGERY—

They can take the fat from your rear and use it to bang out dents in your face. Now that's what I call recycling. It gives a whole new meaning to dancing cheek to cheek.

—*Anita Wise*

A forty-five-year-old woman who has had a face lift doesn't look twenty-five. If it works, she looks like a well-rested forty-three-year-old woman. If it doesn't work, she looks like a Halloween costume.

—*Fran Lebowitz*

The thought of surgery to suck fat out of my body makes me feel sick.
I could never do it.
Instead of liposuction,
why not go directly to the source?
I'd rather have Fridge-o-suction.
Please. Instead of needless surgery just suck the food right out of my refrigerator before it even lands on me.

—Flash Rosenberg

I don't plan to grow old gracefully.
I plan to have face-lifts till my ears meet.

—*Rita Rudner*

If losing your head is a be-heading,
is liposuction a be-hinding?

—*Flash Rosenberg*

—CRIME—

I didn't steal this.
It was "differently acquired."

—Sara Cytron

—CYNICISM—

No matter how cynical you get,
it's impossible to keep up.

—Lily Tomlin

Today is the first day
of the wreck of your life.

—*Becky Burke*

Things are going to get a lot worse
before they get worse.

—*Lily Tomlin*

I live in Ithaca, a small town that seems oh-so-much-smaller when I realize that most of the single males are under twenty-two. Not that I mind the age difference, but I have this silly rule—
I won't fool around with someone I could have given birth to.

—Maxine Wilkie

I once dated a guy who was so dumb
he couldn't count to twenty-one
unless he was naked.

—*Joan Rivers*

When I was seventeen years old I was going
out with a fifty-nine year-old man.
Sexually, we got along great because
the things he couldn't do anymore were
the things I didn't know about.

—*Carol Henry*

My grandmother's ninety. She's dating.
He's ninety-three. It's going great.
They never argue. They can't hear each other.

—*Cathy Ladman*

I don't understand when people say a lover
is "too old" or "too young." As far as I'm
concerned, ANYONE who is on the planet
the same time you are is fair game.

—*Flash Rosenberg*

I went out with a guy who told me
he didn't like women who were sensitive
or vulnerable...so I stabbed him.

—*Karen Rontowski*

Boys don't make passes
at female smart asses.

—*Letty Cottin Pogrebin*

I've figured out why first dates don't work any better than they do. It's because they take place in restaurants. Women are weird and confused and unhappy about food, and men are weird and confused and unhappy about money, yet off they go, the minute they meet, to where you use money to buy food.

—*Adair Lara*

How many of you ever started
dating someone because you were too lazy
to commit suicide?

—*Judy Tenuta*

This guy says, "I'm perfect for you, 'cause
I'm a cross between a macho and a sensitive
man." I said, "Oh, a gay trucker?"

—*Judy Tenuta*

—DEATH—

Final Exit, the suicide how-to book, was a
best-seller for nineteen weeks after its publication.
One year later, the paperback version came out and
did a brisk business. Our questions: Who waited
for the paperback? And what did the self-
destructive cheapskates do with their savings?

—101 Reasons Why We're Doomed
by Meredith Anthony & Alison Power

We're all cremated equal.

—Jane Ace

The dying process begins
the minute we are born,
but it accelerates during dinner parties.
—*Carol Matthau*

They say you shouldn't say nothing
about the dead unless it's good.
He's dead. Good.
—*Moms Mabley*

I've been on a constant diet
for the last two decades.
I've lost a total
of 789 pounds.
By all accounts, I should be
hanging from a charm bracelet.

—Erma Bombeck

—DENTISTS —

I ran into my dentist. At first I didn't know it was him. But then I looked up his nose.

—*Judy Tenuta*

—DIETING—

I bought a talking refrigerator that said "Oink" every time I opened the door. It made me hungry for pork chops.

—*Marie Mott*

The only way to lose weight is
to check it as airline baggage.

—Peggy Ryan

Food is like sex: when you abstain,
even the worst stuff begins to look good.

—Beth McCollister

A great many people in Los Angeles are on strict diets that restrict their intake of synthetic foods. The reason for this appears to be a widely-held belief that organically grown fruit and vegetables make the cocaine work faster.

—*Fran Lebowitz*

I got so depressed about dieting that I had to see a doctor. He said, "For God's sake, pull yourself together." He was trying to get me through the door.

—*Florence Small*

A waist
is a terrible thing
to mind.

—Jane Caminos

I've decided that perhaps I'm bulimic
and just keep forgetting to purge.

—*Paula Poundstone*

—DISABILITY—

My cousin died. He was a dyslexic policeman
who had a heart attack. They found him
by the phone trying to dial 119.

—*Joan Rivers*

When I was young, I was put in a school
for retarded kids for two years before they
realized I actually had a hearing loss...
and they called me slow!

—*Kathy Buckley*

I came into the world this way.
So it's no big deal.
It's not like I wake up every morning and say
"Oh my God! I've got cerebral palsy again!"

—*Geri Jewell*

I dated a producer about five years ago and wanted to impress him. So I told him I didn't really have cerebral palsy. I just said I was having a continuous orgasm. The funny thing is he never knew whether I was coming or going.

—*Geri Jewell*

You know the hardest thing about having cerebral palsy and being a woman? It's plucking my eyebrows. That's how I originally got pierced ears.

—*Geri Jewell*

—DIVORCE—

There is so little difference between husbands, you might as well keep the first.

—Adela Rogers St. Johns

I never even believed in divorce until
after I got married.
—*Diane Ford*

The wages of sin is alimony.
—*Carolyn Wells*

When I'm dating I look at a guy and wonder,
"Is this the man I want my children
to spend their weekends with?"

—*Rita Rudner*

—DOCTORS—

A male gynecologist is like an auto mechanic
who never owned a car.

—*Carrie Snow*

Dermatologists make rash judgments.

—*Patricia Majewski*

—DOGS—

Pugs are living proof that
God has a sense of humor.

—*Margo Kaufman*

I've been SOBER a while. To me, SOBER stands for "Son-of-a-Bitch, Everything's Real!"

—Kathy G

One more drink and
I'll be under the host.

—*Dorothy Parker*

I don't drink or do any drugs. I never have
and I never will. I don't need them.
I'm a Black woman from the land of the free,
home of the brave and I figure
I don't need another illusion.

—*Bertice Berry*

Alcoholism isn't a spectator sport.
Eventually the whole family gets to play.
—*Joyce Rebeta-Burditt*

They're trying to put warning labels on
liquor. "Caution: Alcohol can be dangerous
to pregnant women." That's ironic.
If it weren't for alcohol, most women
wouldn't even be that way.
—*Rita Rudner*

—DRIVING—

Naples traffic isn't a condition.
It's a war in progress.
—Erma Bombeck

My license plate says PMS.
Nobody cuts me off.
—Wendy Liebman

I read Shakespeare and the Bible and I can shoot dice. That's what I call a liberal education.

—Tallulah Bankhead

—EGO—

Listen,
everyone is entitled to my opinion.
—*Madonna*

Egotism—
usually just a case of mistaken nonentity.
—*Barbara Stanwyck*

Success didn't spoil me;
I've always been insufferable.
—*Fran Lebowitz*

It takes a lot of time to be a genius—
you have to sit around so much doing nothing,
really nothing.
—*Gertrude Stein*

He was the most self-involved guy I ever met in my life. He had a coffee mug on his table that said, "I'm the greatest." He had a plaque on the wall that said, "I'm number one." And on his bedspread it said, "The Best." In the middle of making love he said, "Move over—you're getting in my way."

—*Karen Haber*

—ENVIRONMENT—

The other day I bought a wastebasket and carried it home in a paper bag. And when I got home I put the paper bag in the wastebasket.

—*Lily Tomlin*

I live in New York.
I have a new apartment
with French doors in the
bedroom. They don't open
unless I lick them.

—*Judy Gold*

—EXERCISE—

I have to exercise in the morning before
my brain figures out what I'm doing.
—*Marsha Doble*

I really don't think I need buns of steel.
I'd be happy with buns of cinnamon.
—*Ellen DeGeneres*

I don't think jogging is healthy, especially morning jogging. If morning joggers knew how tempting they looked to morning motorists, they would stay home and do sit-ups.

—*Rita Rudner*

My grandmother started walking five miles a day when she was sixty. She's ninety-three today and we don't know where the hell she is.

—*Ellen DeGeneres*

I've been doing leg lifts faithfully for about fifteen years, and the only thing that has gotten thinner is the carpet where I have been doing the leg lifts.

—*Rita Rudner*

I'd say, "It's a Buttmaster, your holiness."

—*Exercise equipment spokesperson Suzanne Somers on how she'd pitch her latest device to the Pope*

They kept telling us
we had to get in touch with our bodies.
Mine isn't all that communicative but
I heard from it on Tuesday morning
when I genially proposed, "Body,
how'd you like to go to the nine o'clock
class in vigorous toning with
resistence?" Clear as a bell my body
said, "Listen, bitch, do it and you die."

—Molly Ivins

—EXPERIENCE—

Keep a diary and one day it'll keep you.

—*Mae West*

A girl can wait for the right man to come along but in the meantime that still doesn't mean she can't have a wonderful time with all the wrong ones.

—*Cher*

To err is human but it feels divine.

—*Mae West*

I'm an experienced woman;
I've been around...Well, all right, I might
not've been around, but I've been...nearby.

—*Mary Richards,* The Mary Tyler Moore Show

My heart is as pure as the driven slush.
—*Tallulah Bankhead*

—FAMILY—

It looks like the "don't ask—don't tell"
policy will go into effect...which,
I believe, is the creed of
dysfunctional families everywhere.
—*Beverly Mickins*

On her proposed Academy Award acceptance speech:

I'd like to thank my mother and my father for providing me with the need to seek the love of strangers.

—*Betsy Salkind*

I've been talking about my family with my
therapist for so long that by now she has her
own problems with these people. Last week,
when I was talking about my mother,
she said, "Look, I don't want to hear a thing
that woman has to say!"

—*Sara Cytron*

My grandmother was a very tough woman.
She buried three husbands.
Two of them were just napping.

—*Rita Rudner*

—FASHION—

Remember that always dressing
in understated good taste is the same
as playing dead.

—*Susan Catherine*

Did you hear about the Scottish drag queen?
He wore pants.

—*Lynn Lavner*

I put on a peekaboo blouse,
he peeked and booed.

—*Phyllis Diller*

It is interesting to speculate how it developed
that in two of the most anti-feminist
institutions, the church and the law court,
the men are wearing dresses.

—*Flo Kennedy*

If men can run the world,
why can't they
stop wearing neckties?
How intelligent is it to
start the day by tying a little
noose around your neck?

—Linda Ellerbee

Although a life-long fashion dropout, I have absorbed enough by reading *Harper's Bazaar* while waiting at the dentist's to have grasped that the purpose of fashion is to make A Statement. My own modest Statement, discerned by true cognoscenti, is, "Woman Who Wears Clothes So She Won't Be Naked."

—*Molly Ivins*

If you are all wrapped up in yourself,
you are overdressed.

—*Kate Halverson*

Why is it considered seductive for women to wear beautiful clothes? Wouldn't it make more sense to wear something so ugly that a guy couldn't wait to take it off you?

—*Flash Rosenberg*

It's my least favorite season of the year...bathing suit season. I don't know why we can't all be shaped like those eighteen-year-old boys they design those suits for.

—*Diane Ford*

When a waiter at Buckingham Palace spilled soup on her dress: Never darken my Dior again!

—Beatrice Lillie

Now they're advertising breathable panty liners. You know some man invented that product. No woman would be inventing a panty liner and putting little holes in there. She'd put little tongues in there.

—Diane Ford

Fashion tells us that women's bodies are not supposed to be shaped like women's bodies, except during sex.

—Julia Willis

If gentlemen prefer Hanes,
why don't they wear them?

—*Judith Sloan*

I do not believe in God.
I believe in cashmere.

—*Fran Lebowitz*

Q: Is lesbian dating an oxymoron?
A: No, but lesbian fashion is!

—*Lea Delaria*

My sister has a social conscience now.
She still wears her fur coat, but across the
back she's embroidered a sampler that says
"Rest in Peace."

—*Julia Willis*

It costs a lot of money
to look this cheap.
—*Dolly Parton*

It's not true I had nothing on.
I had the radio on.
—*Marilyn Monroe*

I miss the good old days
when guys wore
open shirts, gold chains
and polyester suits.
I met many men
I was attracted to.
Okay, so it was static cling.

—Karen Silver

Your right to wear a mint-green polyester
leisure suit ends where it meets my eye.

—*Fran Lebowitz*

This wedding dress cost almost $2,000.
You're supposed to wear it once? Bullshit!
I wear it to work, to the toilet.

—*Claudia Sherman*

A child develops individuality long before he develops taste. I have seen my kid straggle into the kitchen in the morning with outfits that need only one accessory: an empty gin bottle.

—*Erma Bombeck*

Is it okay to hate men but dress just like them?

—*Karen Ripley*

—FEAR—

Considering how dangerous everything is,
nothing is frightening.

—*Gertrude Stein*

—FEMINISM—

If you're not a feminist,
you're a masochist.

—*Gloria Steinem*

The forces in the White House want Hillary to tone down? From what? Did I miss her crazed leather-biker-chick period?

—Beverly Mickins

Nancy Reagan has agreed to be
the first artificial heart donor.

—*Andrea Michaels*

—FOOD—

Q: What's an Irish-Jewish seven course meal?
A: A latke and a six-pack.

—*Caryn Leschen*

Why does Sea World have a seafood
restaurant? I'm halfway through
my fishburger and I realize "Oh my God—
I could be eating a slow learner..."
—*Lynda Montgomery*

I'm a Jewish girl who was raised in
a vegetarian family. My dream is to open
a restaurant called "Soy Vey."
—*Margo Black*

Order me anything out of season.
—*Fannie Brice*

Seize the moment.
Remember all those women on the Titanic
who waved off the dessert cart.
—*Erma Bombeck*

*I try to fill the emptiness
deep inside me with Cheetos,
but I am still depressed.
Only now my fingers
are stained orange.
I am blue.
And I am orange.*

—Karen Salmansohn

Food is an important part
of a balanced diet.

—*Fran Lebowitz*

I tried Flintstones vitamins.
I didn't feel any better but
I could stop the car with my feet.

—*Joan St. Onge*

You've buttered your bread,
now sleep in it.

—*Gracie Allen*

This recipe is certainly silly.
It says to separate two eggs, but it doesn't say
how far to separate them.

—*Gracie Allen*

It's so beautifully arranged on the plate—
you know someone's fingers
have been all over it.

—*Julia Child*

Forget the withered rose or faded vow from
Mr. Right. Love departs—but sauerkraut,
once savored, stays the night.

—*Barbara J. Petoskey*

When I buy cookies I just eat four and throw the rest away. But first I spray them with Raid so I won't dig them out of the garbage later. Be careful, though, because that Raid really doesn't taste that bad.

—Janette Barber

I had left home (like all Jewish girls) in order to eat pork and take birth control pills. When I first shared an intimate evening with my husband, I was swept away by the passion (so dormant inside myself) of a long and tortured existence. The physical cravings I had tried so hard to deny, finally and ultimately sated....But enough about the pork.

—*Roseanne*

—FRIENDSHIP—

A friend is someone you don't have to talk to anymore once the food is on the table.

—*Sabrina Matthews*

When I was a girl I had only two friends, and they were imaginary. And they would only play with each other.

—*Rita Rudner*

Q: What can you give a friend who has everything?
A: Shelves.

—*Patty Marx*

Laugh and the world laughs with you.
Cry and you cry with your girlfriends.

—*Laurie Kuslansky*

—FUN—

Instant gratification takes too long.

—*Carrie Fisher*

*If only we'd stop
trying to be happy
we could have
a pretty good time.*
—Edith Wharton

A desire to have all the fun is nine-tenths
of the law of chivalry.

—*Dorothy Sayers*

Too much of a good thing
can be wonderful.

—*Mae West*

—GAMES—

It's not whether you win or lose—
it's how you lay the blame.
—Fran Lebowitz

I figure you have the same chance of winning
the lottery whether you play or not.
—Fran Lebowitz

—GARDENING—

Perennials are the ones that grow like weeds,
biennials are the ones that die this year
instead of next, and hardy annuals are
the ones that never come up at all.

—*Katharine Whitehorn*

—GOSSIP—

If you can't say anything good about
someone, sit right here by me.

—*Alice Roosevelt Longsworth*

I hate
to spread rumors—
but what else
can one do with them?

—*Amanda Lear*

—GYNECOLOGY—

I got a postcard from my gynecologist. It said "Did you know it's time for your annual checkup?" No, but now my mailman does.

—*Cathy Ladman*

—HAIR—

Guys are lucky because they get to grow moustaches. I wish I could. It's like having a little pet for your face.

—*Anita Wise*

I refuse to think of them as chin hairs.
I think of them as stray eyebrows.

—*Janette Barber*

I've been in this hair change mode for
several years—it grows from a fear that
I will end up like Margaret Mead or Mamie
Eisenhower and adopt a style in my twenties,
stick with it no matter what, and look like
a clown with a danish on my head at seventy.

—*Maxine Wilkie*

The heck with the natural look. After all, you can't take credit for what you're born with, only for what you do yourself. Where would Marilyn Monroe be if she'd clung to the hair color God gave her? We'd have a movie called "Gentlemen Prefer Mousy Brown Hair."

—*Adair Lara*

I'm worried that my hair is going to get bigger than I am and take me places I don't want to go.

—*Jennifer Heath*

I happen to have weird hair which is why I don't dress up fancy. If I dress up, people just look at me and go, "Oooh, look at her head." This way here, it's more of a total look and nobody can put their finger on quite what they think is wrong.

—Paula Poundstone

—HALLOWEEN—

A fine American tradition of teaching our children
to beg door-to-door dressed as mass murderers
and codependent women. The planning takes
weeks, but it's worth it just to see how lively
a four-year-old can get after mainlining Milk Duds
for three hours.

—*Cathy Crimmins*

—HEALTH—

Happiness is good health and a bad memory.

—*Ingrid Bergma*

Health—what my friends are always drinking to before they fall down.

—*Phyllis Diller*

Never go to a doctor
whose office plants have died.

—*Erma Bombeck*

Life is drab unless we make the most of each new experience. Should sickness be an exception? If you want to live life to the fullest, why not glorify each symptom and dramatize each twinge? Don't just sit there— worry about your health.

—*Carol L. King*

—HELL—

My idea of hell is to be stranded on a desert island with nothing to read but Anais Nin's diaries.

—*Katha Pollitt*

—HOME—

Home is a great place—
after all the other places have closed.
—*Texas Guinan*

—HOUSEKEEPING—

My second favorite household chore is
ironing. My first being hitting my head
on the top bunk bed until I faint.
—*Erma Bombeck*

I'm a wonderful housekeeper.
Every time I get divorced,
I keep the house.

—*Zsa Zsa Gabor*

A dish that don't survive the dishwasher
don't deserve to live.

—*Liz Scott*

Don't cook. Don't clean. No man will ever make love to a woman because she waxed the linoleum—"My God, the floor's immaculate. Lie down, you hot bitch."

—*Joan Rivers*

I don't buy temporary insanity as a murder defense. Breaking into someone's home and ironing all their clothes is temporary insanity.

—*Sue Kolinsky*

I prefer the word homemaker, because housewife always implies that there may be a wife someplace else.

—Bella Abzug

I would rather lie on a sofa
than sweep beneath it.
—*Shirley Conran*

Nature abhors a vacuum.
And so do I.
—*Anne Gibbons*

Cleaning your home while your kids are still
growing is like shovelling the walk before
it stops snowing.

—*Phyllis Diller*

If you want to get rid of stinking odors
in the kitchen, stop cooking.

—*Erma Bombeck*

I know people who are so clean you can eat off their floors. You can't eat off my table. Fang, my husband, says the only thing domestic about me is that I was born in this country.

—*Phyllis Diller*

—HUMOR—

Comedy is half music.

—*Joan Rivers*

If evolution was worth its salt, by now it should've evolved something better than survival of the fittest...I think a better idea would be survival of the wittiest.

—Jane Wagner

Comedy is tragedy,
plus time.
—*Carol Burnett*

Humor is just truth,
only faster!
—*Gilda Radner*

—HUNTERS—

I ask people why they have deer heads on their walls. They always say, "Because it's such a beautiful animal." There you go! I think my mother is attractive, but I have photographs of her.

—*Ellen DeGeneres*

—INFORMATION—

Everybody gets so much information all day long that they lose their common sense.

—*Gertrude Stein*

—ILLNESS—

I'm starting to worry more about getting
Alzheimer's than AIDS...
but for the life of me, I can't remember why.

—Anita Milner

—INNER CHILDREN—

I've been having kind of a difficult day...my
Inner Child threw up on my Higher Power.

—Lynn Lavner

—INNER PEACE—

There is no such thing as inner peace. There is only nervousness and death.

—Fran Lebowitz

—INSULTS—

You remind me of my brother Bosco—
only he had a human head.

—*Judy Tenuta*

About another actress: She's the original
good time that was had by all.

—*Bette Davis*

Who lit the fuse on your tampon?
—*button*

—JEWELRY—

My husband gave me a necklace. It's fake.
I requested fake. Maybe I'm paranoid,
but in this day and age, I don't want
something around my neck that's worth
more than my head.

—*Rita Rudner*

—JOURNALISM—

Journalism is the ability to meet
the challenge of filling space.

—*Rebecca West*

You should always believe all you read
in the newspapers, as this makes them
more interesting.

—*Rose Maccaulay*

—JUSTICE—

Juries scare me.
I don't want to put
my fate in the hands of
twelve people who
weren't even smart enough
to get out of jury duty.

—Monica Piper

No good deed goes unpunished.

—*Claire Boothe Luce*

—LAUGHTER—

Laugh and the world laughs with you;
cry and the world laughs at you.

—*Caryn Leschen*

Laugh and the world laughs with you.
Stub your toe and the world laughs
whether you do or not.

—*Linda Perret's Humor Files*

It's no laughing matter,
but it doesn't matter if you laugh.

—*Jennie Gudmundsen*

—LAWYERS—

My father was a criminal lawyer.
There are some people who will tell you
that's redundant.

—*Lynn Lavner*

I don't believe man
is woman's natural enemy.
Perhaps his lawyer is.

—*Shana Alexander*

—LESBIANS AND GAYS—

Remember the TV coverage of the Gulf War? CNN kept showing the one straight woman over there. Every hour on the hour, they'd haul her out and they'd say, "This is Captain Mary Smith and she wants to say 'hi' to her husband, Mark, and her son, Johnny." Meanwhile, there's two thousand dykes standing behind her saying, "Hey, Marge, keep my bowling ball polished, OK?"

—Robin Tyler

If we wanted to be part of an institution that
is hostile to gays and women,
we'd just stay home with our families.
—*Georgia Ragsdale*

My lesbianism is an act of Christian charity.
All those women out there are praying for
a man, and I'm giving them my share.
—*Rita Mae Brown*

I'm a little bit femme and a little bit butch.
I wear makeup…but I keep it in a tackle box.

—*Lynda Montgomery*

Q: How do people get to be homosexual?
A: Homosexuals are chosen first on talent,
then interview, and then the swimsuit
and evening gown competitions…

—*Suzanne Westenhoefer*

I'm out to everybody in my family,
except my aunt. She's agoraphobic,
and I figure if she won't come out for me,
why should I come out for her?

—*Lynda Montgomery*

If male homosexuals are called "gay,"
then female homosexuals should
be called "ecstatic."

—*Shelly Roberts*

The Bible contains six admonishments to homosexuals and 362 admonishments to heterosexuals. That doesn't mean that God doesn't love heterosexuals. It's just that they need more supervision.

—Lynn Lavner

Parents should be reminded,
gently and often, that, "I love you anyway,"
is not a compliment.

—*Shelly Roberts*

When the family first comes to visit,
what I did was "de-dyke" the apartment.
We call it "straightening up."

—*Kate Clinton*

I wear a T-shirt that says
"The family tree stops here."
—*Suzanne Westenhoefer*

I'm out,
therefore I am.
—*Ursula Roma*

Q: What do homosexuals do in bed?
A: It's a lot like heterosexual sex, only one of us doesn't have to fake orgasm.

—*Suzanne Westenhoefer*

A lesbian is any uppity woman, regardless of sexual preference. If they don't call you a lesbian, you're probably not accomplishing anything.

—*Cheris Kramarae & Paula Treichler*

I can close my eyes and still hear my mother's voice saying, "Always remember, it's just as easy to fall in love with a rich girl as with a poor one." Of course, she was talking to my brother at the time.

—Lynn Lavner

—LIFE—

Life is short, but it's wide.

—Jennifer Unlimited

Most of us live our lives devoid
of cinematic moments.

—Nora Ephron

Your life story would not make a good book.
Don't even try.

—*Fran Lebowitz*

Life's a bitch and then they call you one.

—*Mary Frances Connelly*

Anybody who thinks they
know everything ain't been around
long enough to know anything.

—*Gladiola Montana*

I try to take one day at a time,
but sometimes several days
attack me at once.

—*Jennifer Unlimited*

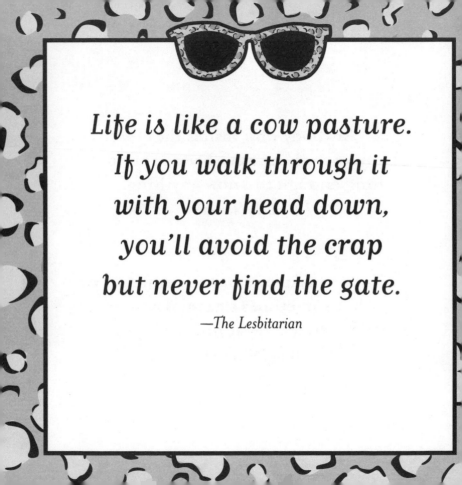

*Life is like a cow pasture.
If you walk through it
with your head down,
you'll avoid the crap
but never find the gate.*

—*The Lesbitarian*

Inside every older person is a younger person wondering what happened.

—*Jennifer Unlimited*

I've always said that I wanted to find myself before somebody bigger did.

—*Carrie Fisher*

I haven't known what to do for so long,
I'm getting good at it.

—*Flash Rosenberg*

Life is something to do
when you can't get to sleep.

—*Fran Lebowitz*

If I had to live my life again,
I'd make all the same mistakes—
only sooner.

—*Tallulah Bankhead*

They say the movies should be more like life.
I think life
should be more like the movies.

—*Myrna Loy*

It is not true
that life is one damn thing
after another—
it's one damn thing
over and over.

—*Edna St. Vincent Millay*

If you can't be a good example, then
you'll just have to be a horrible warning.

—*Catherine Aird*

—LITERATURE—

Everywhere I go I'm asked if I think
universities stifle writers. My opinion is that
they don't stifle enough of them.

—*Flannery O'Connor*

I think Phillip Roth is a great writer.
But I wouldn't want to shake his hand.

—*Jacqueline Susann*

The difference between owning a book
and borrowing a book is that when
you own it you can get food on it.

—*Susan Catherine*

This is not a novel to be tossed lightly aside.
It should be thrown with great force.

—*Dorothy Parker*

I have only read one book in my life, and
that is *White Fang*. It's so frightfully good
I've never bothered to read another.

—*Nancy Mitford*

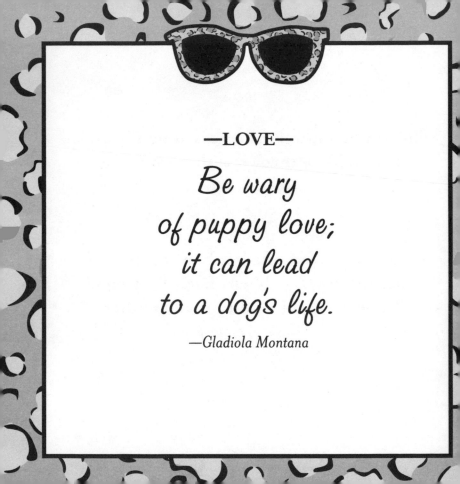

—LOVE—

*Be wary
of puppy love;
it can lead
to a dog's life.*

—Gladiola Montana

"I love you" is not a question.
—*Shelly Roberts*

Love conquers all things
except poverty and a toothache.
—*Mae West*

If love is the answer,
could you please rephrase the question?

—Lily Tomlin

—MANNERS—

Familiarity doesn't breed contempt;
it is contempt.

—Florence King

It's all right for a perfect stranger to kiss your hand as long as he's perfect.

—*Mae West*

—MAKEUP—

Makeup is such a weird concept, but I buy into it like every woman I know. I'll wake up in the morning and look in the mirror: "Gee, I really don't look so good. Maybe if my eyelids were blue, I'd be more attractive...."

—*Cathy Ladman*

—MARRIAGE—

After a few years of marriage a man can look right at a woman without seeing her and a woman can see right through a man without looking at him.

—Helen Rowland

In August, my husband and I celebrated our 38th wedding anniversary. You know what I finally realized? If I had killed that man the first time I thought about it, I'd have been out of jail by now.

—*Anita Milner*

A wedding is just like a funeral except that you get to smell your own flowers.

—*Grace Hansen*

Before accepting a marriage proposal,
take a good look at his father.
If he's still handsome, witty, and has
all his teeth…marry him instead.

—*Diane Jordan*

It's ridiculous to think you can spend
your entire life with just one person.
Three is about the right number.

—*Clare Boothe Luce*

I've married
a few people I shouldn't have,
but haven't we all?

—*Mamie Van Doren*

A girl must marry for love,
and keep on marrying until she finds it.

—*Zsa Zsa Gabor*

The trouble with
some women is that
they get all excited
about nothing—
and then marry him.

—Cher

Marriage is a souvenir of love.

—*Helen Rowland*

Bigamy is having one husband too many.
Monogamy is the same.

—*Erica Jong*

The surest way to be alone is to get married.

—*Gloria Steinem*

The only thing that keeps me from
being happily married...is my husband.

—*Andra Douglas*

Getting married is a lot like getting into
a tub of hot water. After you get used to it,
it ain't so hot.

—*Minnie Pearl*

Marrying a man is like buying something
you've been admiring for a long time
in a shop window. You may love it when you
get it home, but it doesn't always go
with everything else.

—*Jean Kerr*

Any woman who
still thinks marriage is
a fifty-fifty proposition is
only proving that
she doesn't understand
either men or percentages.

—*Flo Kennedy*

Marriage is a great institution,
but I'm not ready for an institution yet.

—*Mae West*

I married beneath me—
all women do.

—*Nancy Astor*

The old theory was "Marry an older man, because they're more mature." But the new theory is "Men don't mature. Marry a younger one."

—*Rita Rudner*

Some of us are becoming the men we wanted to marry.

—*Gloria Steinem*

A man in love is incomplete
until he's married—then he's finished.
—*Zsa Zsa Gabor*

I'm thirty-three, single...Don't you think it's
a generalization you should be married at
thirty-three? That's like looking at
somebody who's seventy and saying "Hey,
when are you gonna break your hip?
All your friends are breaking
their hips—what are you waiting for?"
—*Sue Kolinsky*

I haven't known
any open marriages,
although quite a few
have been ajar.

—Zsa Zsa Gabor

To George Burns: George, you're too old to get married again. Not only can't you cut the mustard, honey, you're too old to open the jar.

—*La Wanda Page*

Trust your husband, adore your husband, and get as much as you can in your own name.

—*Joan Rivers*

When asked why she had never married:
I can't mate in captivity.

—*Gloria Steinem*

—MASTECTOMY—

On learning she needed a mastectomy:
I thought of the thousands of luncheons and dinners I had attended where they slapped a name tag on my left bosom. I always smiled and said, "Now, what shall we name the other one?" That would no longer be a problem.

—*Erma Bombeck*

A few weeks after my surgery, I went out to play catch with my golden retriever. When I bent over to pick up the ball, my prothesis fell out. The dog snatched it, and I found myself chasing him down the road yelling "Hey, come back here with my breast!"

—*Linda Ellerbee*

—MATURITY—

Old age ain't no place for sissies.

—*Bette Davis*

I don't know how
you feel about old age...
but in my case
I didn't even see it coming.
It hit me from the rear.

—*Phyllis Diller*

Thirty-five is when you finally get your head together and your body starts falling apart.

—*Caryn Leschen*

Don't think of it as wrinkles.
Think of it as relaxed-fit skin.

—*Cathy Crimmins*

The good thing about going to your
twenty-five-year high school reunion is that
you get to see all your old classmates.
The bad thing is that they get to see you.

—*Anita Milner*

You can't stay young forever, but you can be
immature for the rest of your life.

—*Maxine Wilkie*

Old age is like a plane flying through
a storm. Once you're aboard,
there's nothing you can do.

—*Golda Meir*

The older one grows,
the more one likes indecency.

—*Virginia Woolf*

*The older I get,
the simpler the definition of
maturity seems: it's the
length of time between when
I realize someone is a jackass
and when I tell them
that they're one.*

—Brett Butler

Don't get upset about wrinkles:
they're just foreshadowing.
—*Cathy Crimmins*

—MEDITATION—

I've taken up meditation. I like to have an
espresso first to make it more challenging.
—*Betsy Salkind*

—MEN—

I want a man who's kind and understanding.
Is that too much to ask of a millionaire?

—Zsa Zsa Gabor

Fooling a man ain't all that hard.
Finding one that ain't a fool is a lot harder.

—Gladiola Montana

There's a commercial where guys sit around
drinking beer, cleaning fish, wiping
their noses on their sleeves and saying
"It doesn't get any better than this."
That's not a commercial. That's a warning.

—*Diane Jordan*

A woman needs a man
like a fish needs a net.

—*Cynthia Heimel*

*A man's got to do
what a man's got to do.
A woman must do
what he can't.*

—*Rhonda Hansome*

Why can't men get more in touch with their feminine side and become self-destructive?

—*Betsy Salkind*

There are a lot of nice-looking guys out there tonight. But I know no matter how cute and sexy these guys are, there's always someone somewhere who's sick of them.

—*Carol Henry*

A good man doesn't just happen. They have to be created by us women. A guy is a lump like a doughnut. So, first you gotta get rid of all the stuff his mom did to him, and then you gotta get rid of all that macho crap that they pick up from the beer commercials. And then there's my personal favorite, the male ego.

—*Roseanne*

Macho does not prove mucho.

—*Zsa Zsa Gabor*

Personally, I think if a woman hasn't met
the right man by the time she's twenty-four,
she may be lucky.

—*Deborah Kerr*

It is possible that blondes
also prefer gentlemen.

—*Mamie Van Doren*

Beware of men who cry. It's true that men who cry are sensitive to and in touch with feelings, but the only feelings they tend to be sensitive to and in touch with are their own.

—Nora Ephron

A woman is a woman until the day she dies,
but a man's a man only as long as he can.
—*Moms Mabley*

If they can put one man on the moon
why can't they put them all there?
—*Chocolate Waters*

Q: Can you imagine a world without men?
A: No crime, and lots of happy fat women.

—*Nicole Hollander*

Men won't stop and ask for directions
because driving is too much like sex: they
can't stop until they get where they're going.

—*Diane Jordan*

Men can read maps better than women.
'Cause only the male mind could conceive
of one inch equaling a hundred miles.

—*Roseanne*

Don't accept rides from strange men—
and remember that all men
are strange as hell.

—*Robin Morgan*

—MENSTRUATION—

*Periods are like
airplane food.
You don't want it,
but if yours doesn't come,
you go, "Where's mine?"*

—Bertice Berry

A period is just the beginning
of a lifelong sentence.
—*Cathy Crimmins*

Every month he asks me if I've got
"the curse." So, finally, I told him,
"I must. I'm living with you, aren't I?"
—*Stephanie Piro*

I would like it if men had to partake in the same hormonal cycles to which we're subjected monthly. Maybe that's why men declare war—because they have a need to bleed on a regular basis.

—*Brett Butler*

My doctor said, "I've got good news and I've got bad news. The good news is you don't have premenstrual syndrome. The bad news is—you're a bitch!"

—*Rhonda Bates*

—MENTAL HEALTH —

Everybody says that having multiple personality
disorder is so terrible. I don't think having
ninety-two personalities is so terrible. I think
it's wonderful because I know so
many people who don't even have one.

—*Suzy Berger*

Codependents' Support Group:
"Let's help each other
to stop helping each other!"

—*Laura Ardiel*

The statistics on sanity
are that one out of every
four Americans is suffering
from some form of mental illness.
Think of your three best friends.
If they are okay,
then it's you.

—Rita Mae Brown

—MIDLIFE CRISIS—

The cup isn't half empty—it's evaporating!
—*Alice Kahn*

The midlife crisis usually begins with a checkup at
the doctor's. You feel you are in perfect health.
And you are. It's just that you suddenly realize the
doctor is some punk kid. You can no longer call
him Dr. Silverstein. Instead, you say, "Do you
know a damn thing about systemic yeast, Sean?"
—*Alice Kahn*

Menopausal Women Nostalgic For Choice

—bumper sticker

—MOBILE HOMES—

Have you ever noticed that people in mobile home parks never, ever move? I mean look, folks, if you are going to live in the same place for fifty years, get rid of the wheels.

—Shashi Bhatia

—MONEY—

Does giving birth make me a real woman?
No, earning less than a man
makes me a real woman.

—Suzy Berger

I've been sort of crabby lately.
It's that time of month again—
the rent's due.

—Margaret Smith

If you are truly serious about preparing your child for the future, don't teach him to subtract— teach him to deduct.

—Fran Lebowitz

At the parking garage the sign says,
"Lost Tickets Pay Max."
What a great deal for Max!

—*Flash Rosenberg*

I do want to get rich but I never want to do
what there is to do to get rich.

—*Gertrude Stein*

I don't want to make money.
I just want to be wonderful.

—*Marilyn Monroe*

If this man had not twelve thousand a year,
he would be a very stupid fellow.

—*Jane Austen*

The most beautiful words in the
English language are "check enclosed."
—*Dorothy Parker*

I don't buy all this news of a rebounding
economy. Just the other day my best friend
had a nose job—and twelve people applied.
—*Mary Jo Crowley*

The way I look at it,
if the kids are still alive
when my husband comes
home from work,
then I've done my job.

—*Roseanne*

Money is always there,
but the pockets change.

—*Gertrude Stein*

—MOTHERHOOD—

Never lend your car to anyone to whom
you have given birth.

—*Erma Bombeck*

A woman came to ask the doctor if a woman should have children after thirty-five.
I said thirty-five is enough for any woman!

—*Gracie Allen*

It's not easy being a mother. If it were easy, fathers would do it.

—*Dorothy*, The Golden Girls

I was on a corner the other day when a wild-looking sort of gypsy-looking lady with a dark veil over her face grabbed me right on Ventura Boulevard and said, "Karen Haber! You're never going to find happiness, and no one is ever going to marry you." I said, "Mom, leave me alone."

—*Karen Huber*

Children use up the same part of my head as poetry does.

—*Libby Houston*

My mother says she just
wants me to be happy—
doing what
she wants me to do.

—*Julia Willis*

How is a kid going to develop lung power if every little whimper makes Mom come running? My recommendation: keep the baby monitor you got as a gift and put it under the guest bed—lots more fun!

—*Cathy Crimmins*

I don't have any kids.
Well…at least none that I know about.

—*Carol Leifer*

Never have more children
than you have car windows.

—*Erma Bombeck*

What do you get on Mother's Day if you have
kids? You know what. A card with flowers
that are made out of pink toilet paper—
a lot of pink toilet paper. You get breakfast
in bed. Then you get up and fix everybody
else their breakfast. And then you go to the
bathroom and you are out of toilet paper.

—*Liz Scott*

The phrase "working mother"
is redundant.

—*Jane Sellman*

—MOVIES—

I really detest movies like *Indecent Proposal* and
Pretty Woman because they
send a message to women that sleeping with
a rich man is the ultimate goal—
and really, that's such a small part of it.

—*Laura Kightlinger*

—MUSIC—

On Country music:
I love the sound
of codependence
wafting over the prairie.

—Carol Steinel

I worry that the person who thought up
Muzak may be thinking up something else.

—*Lily Tomlin*

—OPTIMISM—

Hope is the feeling you have that
the feeling you have isn't permanent.

—*Jean Kerr*

"I'm going to be a big star!" In California, we call that sort of statement "creative visualization." In the other forty-nine states, it's called self-delusion.

—*Maureen Brownsey*

—PEOPLE—

There's not much good in the worst of us, and so many of the worst of us get the best of us, that the rest of us aren't even worth talking about.

—*Gracie Allen*

What are perfect strangers? Do they have perfect hair? Do they dress perfectly?

—*Ellen DeGeneres*

—PERSONAL ADS—

Personal ads are dangerous. You have to separate the ones who are lying from the ones who are hallucinating.

—*Rita Rudner*

*Sometimes
I worry about being
a success
in a mediocre world.*

—Lily Tomlin

Ignorance is no excuse—
it's the real thing.

—*Irene Peter*

If you can keep your head while all about you
are losing theirs, it's just possible
you haven't grasped the situation.

—*Jean Kerr*

I had never been as resigned to ready-made
ideas as I was to ready-made clothes,
perhaps because although I couldn't sew,
I could think.

—*Jane Rule*

—POLITICS—

That you can't fight City Hall is a rumor
being circulated by City Hall.

—*Audre Lord*

All politicians are alligators;
they are all alligators.

Billie Carr

As far as the men who are running for
president are concerned,
they aren't even people
I would date.

—*Nora Ephron*

A politician
is a fellow who
will lay down your life
for his country.

—*Texas Guinan*

A recent Ku Klux Klan rally in Austin produced an eccentric counter-demonstration. When the fifty Klansmen appeared...in front of the state capitol, they were greeted by five thousand locals who had turned out for a "Moon the Klan" rally. Citizens dropped trough both singly and in groups, occasionally producing a splendid wave effect.
It was a swell do.

—*Molly Ivins*

A female president—
maybe they'd start calling it the "Ova Office."
—*Brett Butler*

Ninety-eight percent of the adults in this country are decent, hard-working, honest Americans. It's the other lousy two percent that get all the publicity. But then, we elected them.

—*Lily Tomlin*

I am working for the time when unqualified blacks, browns, and women join the unqualified men in running our government.

—*Cissy Farenthold*

Legislators do not merely mix metaphors; they are the Waring blenders of metaphors, the Cuisinarts of the field. By the time you let the head of the camel into the tent, opening a loophole big enough to drive a truck through, you may have thrown the baby out with the bathwater by putting a Band-aid on an open wound, and then you have to turn over the first rock in order to find a sacred cow.

—*Molly Ivins*

The press went tearing off down a very dangerous and stupid path in '88 when they wrote about Hart's affairs. After twenty-five years of watching politics I have never been able to cite any correlation whatever between who these guys screw and how they perform in public office. The question is who they screw in their public capacity.

—Molly Ivins

—PREGNANCY—

If pregnancy were a book,
they would cut the last two chapters.

—*Nora Ephron*

Pregnancy is much like adolescence,
except it's more tiring and you don't get
to leave home when it's over.

—*Cathy Crimmins*

When I was in labor the nurses would look
at me and say, "Do you still think
blondes have more fun?"

—*Joan Rivers*

When I had my baby,
I screamed and screamed. And that was just
during conception.

—*Joan Rivers*

He tricked me into marrying him.
He told me I was pregnant.

—*Carol Leifer*

I told my mother I was going to have
natural childbirth. She said to me, "Linda,
you've been taking drugs all your life.
Why stop now?"

—*Linda Maldonado*

"*Feel the baby kicking, feel the baby kicking,*" says my pregnant friend who is pregnant and deliriously happy about it. To me, life is tough enough without having someone kick you from the inside.

—Rita Rudner

If men could get pregnant,
abortion would be a sacrament.

—*Flo Kennedy*

When a friend gave birth to a child, Dorothy
Parker sent her a congratulatory telegram:
"We all knew you had it in you!"

When I was born, I was so surprised
I couldn't talk for a year and a half.

—*Gracie Allen*

One of my friends told me she was in labor
for thirty-six hours. I don't even want to do
anything that feels good for thirty-six hours.

—*Rita Rudner*

One book recommends choosing a
Birth Mantra to chant over and over again.
I didn't realize until I went into labor that I had
subconsciously chosen my mantra:
"Get This Baby Out Of Me."

—*Cathy Crimmins*

The [pregnancy bathing] suit was the size of
a VW beetle, and black with big white polka dots
all over it. This swimsuit captured that
oh-so-special look at the top of any woman's
fashion agenda: Bozo swallows a watermelon.

—*Cathy Crimmins*

My mother told me, "Judy, you'll never amount to anything because you always procrastinate." I said, "Oh yeah? Just wait!"

—Judy Tenuta

The only thing that has to be finished
by next Tuesday is next Monday.

—*Jennifer Unlimited*

—RACE & ETHNICITY—

Jedda is my real name, and Jones is my
slave name; it belonged to my ex-husband.

—*Jedda Jones*

Men look at me and think I'm going to walk on their backs or something. I tell them, "The only time I'll walk on your back is if there's something on the other side of you that I want."

—*Margaret Cho*

I think we can agree racial prejudice is stupid. Because if you spend time with someone from another race and really get to know them, you can find other reasons to hate them.

—*Bernadette Luckett*

I travel a lot, and every day I'm in a different hotel. For some reason, people mistake me for the maid. The other day this guy says, "You can come into my room and do your job now!" So I went in there and told him some jokes.

—*Bertice Berry*

There is an incredible amount of magic and feistiness in black men that nobody has been able to wipe out. But everybody has tried.

—*Toni Morrison*

I don't look like Whoopi Goldberg. People confuse us because we're both black and have dreadlocks. The other day a lady on the bus said to me, "You look just like Whoopi Goldberg."
I told her, "You're fat and white, but you don't look like Mama Cass!"

—Bertice Berry

My mother's Puerto Rican and my father's
Russian-Jewish so we consider ourselves
to be Jewricans or Puertojews. I think
Puertojew sounds like a kosher bathroom,
so I prefer Jewrican.

—*Rachel Ticotin*

—RAGE—

Never go to bed mad. Stay up and fight.

—*Phyllis Diller*

I read one psychologist's theory that said, "Never strike a child in anger." When could I strike him? When he's kissing me on my birthday? When he is recuperating from measles? Do I slap the Bible out of his hand on a Sunday?

—*Erma Bombeck*

—REALITY—

Every time I close the door on reality it comes in through the windows.

—*Jennifer Unlimited*

I made some studies, and reality is
the leading cause of stress amongst those
in touch with it.

—*Jane Wagner*

In city rooms and in the bars where
newspeople drink, you can find out what's
going on. You can't find it in the papers.

—*Molly Ivins*

—REINCARNATION—

*I don't care about who I was
in a former life. Why waste time
finding out whether
I was Cleopatra or Nefertiti?
I believe it's a much better use of
time to craft my life in the present
ever more passionately. I'd rather
work hard to be Flash Rosenberg
in Someone Else's former life.*

—Flash Rosenberg

You know, I used to believe in
reincarnation, but that was in a past life.

—*Karen Salmansohn*

—RELIGION—

I'm a Catholic. It's a little different being
a black Catholic. The name of my church is
"Our Lady Queen of Soul." We have a big statue of
Aretha Franklin in front of the church.
She's holding the little baby, Stevie Wonder.

—*Jedda Jones*

I recently became a Christian Scientist.
It was the only health plan I could afford.

—*Betsy Salkind*

God is love,
but get it in writing.

—*Gypsy Rose Lee*

All religions are the same: religion is basically guilt, with different holidays.

—*Cathy Ladman*

Q: How do you explain human suffering if there is a God?

A: Shouldn't God be the one explaining?

—*Patty Marx*

When we talk to God,
we're praying.
When God talks to us,
we're schizophrenic.

—Jane Wagner

—ROMANCE—

Treat romance like a cane toad.
Study it furtively—then squash it!
—Kaz Cooke

Remember,
lust makes you stupid.
—Nicole Hollander

Cinderella lied to us. There should be a Betty Ford Center where they deprogram you by putting you in an electric chair, play "Some Day My Prince Will Come" and hit you and go "Nobody's coming… Nobody's coming…Nobody's coming."

—*Judy Carter*

Book title: If You Can't Live Without Me, Why Aren't You Dead Yet?

—*Cynthia Heimel*

—RULES—

If you obey all the rules
you miss all the fun.

—Katherine Hepburn

—SAFETY—

Advice to children crossing the street:
damn the lights. Watch the cars.
The lights ain't never killed nobody.

—Moms Mabley

*Stand firm in your refusal
to remain conscious
during algebra.
In real life, I assure you,
there is no such thing
as algebra.*

—Fran Lebowitz

I majored in nursing but I had to drop it
because I ran out of milk.

—*Judy Tenuta*

—SCIENCE—

The latest scientific studies show that
all mice and rats have cancer.

—*Julia Willis*

The formula for water is H_2O.
Is the formula for an ice cube H_2O squared?

—*Lily Tomlin*

—SEX—

What do partners in a codependent couple
say to each other? "That was wonderful
for you. How was it for me?"

—*Wendy Kaminer*

Sex is a lot harder for men than women. If a man wants a woman to have sex with him, he's got to ask her out, wine her, dine her, drug her up….But if a woman wants a man to have sex with her, all she has to do is ask for a promotion.

—*Robin Greenspan*

Some people say older men have long endurance and can make love longer. Let's think about this. Who wants to fuck an old man for a long time?

—*Marsha Warfield*

Scientists now say
you can get cancer from
the radiation thrown off by
your electric blanket.
I'm so depressed.
Here I am fifty-six years old,
and the most dangerous thing
I've ever done in bed
is turn on the blanket.

—Anita Milner

Of course, I'm sure we all place far too much importance on sex, but it's like an old friend of mine used to say: "When you've seen one, you've seen one."

—*Julia Willis*

If brevity is the soul of wit, your penis must be a riot.

—*Donna Gephart*

On being told that a new male acquaintance was 6' 7":
Let's forget about the six feet
and talk about the seven inches.

—*Mae West*

Freud and Jung broke up over the concept
of penis envy. Freud thought that every
woman wanted a penis. Jung thought that
every woman wanted his penis.

—*Ellen Orchid*

On the *Phil Donahue Show* I saw that many men were impotent. How many men here are impotent?…Oh, you can't get your hands up either?

—*Roseanne*

Your daughter is sixteen years old and sexually active? Do I have any advice? For starters—keep her away from Woody Allen!

—*Lily Tomlin*

I once had a girlfriend who liked sex the best under time pressure—when she had to rush. So we used to pretend that she was an air traffic controller who had ten seconds to come before two jumbo jets would collide in mid-air. That was exciting—the best nine and a half seconds of my life!

—Sara Cytron

If the bedroom were a kitchen,
women would be crockpots and men
would be microwaves.

—*Diana Jordan*

My mom always said men are like linoleum
floors. Lay 'em right and you can walk
all over them for thirty years.

—*Brett Butler*

Doctors say it's okay
to have sex after a heart attack,
provided you close the ambulance door.
—*Phyllis Diller*

About her ex-husband: In lovemaking, what he
lacked in size, he made up for in speed.
—*Roseanne*

I'd get into bondage,
but there are too many strings attached.
—*Donna Gephart*

A hard man is good to find.
—*Mae West*

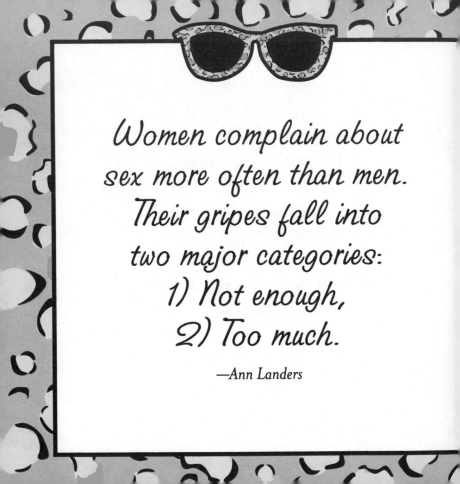

Women complain about sex more often than men. Their gripes fall into two major categories: 1) Not enough, 2) Too much.

—Ann Landers

A healthy sex life.
Best thing in the world for a woman's voice.

—*Leontyne Price*

I understand there's a new edition of *Playboy* magazine designed for married men. Every month the centerfold is the same picture.

—*Mary Jo Crowley*

The important thing in acting
is to be able to laugh and cry.
If I have to cry, I think of my sex life.
If I have to laugh, I think of my sex life.

—*Glenda Jackson*

Sex when you're married is like going
to a 7-11. There's not much variety
but at three in the morning, it's always there.

—*Carol Leifer*

Q: Just how responsible am I
for my partner's orgasm?
A: Well, I guess that depends
on whether or not you're there.

—*Lea Delaria*

Nothing was happening in our marriage.
I nicknamed our waterbed Lake Placid.

—*Phyllis Diller*

Dr. Ruth says we women should tell our lovers how to make love to us. My boyfriend goes nuts if I tell him how to drive!

—Pam Stone

If men really knew how to do it,
they wouldn't have to pay for it.

—*Roseanne*

Q: What do men really like in bed?
A: Breakfast.

—*Nicole Hollander*

How lucky we are that we can reach our genitals instead of that spot on our back that itches.

—*Flash Rosenberg*

We got new advice as to what motivated man to walk upright: to free his hands for masturbation.

—*Jane Wagner*

He just kept rushing through the lovemaking. Which is the part I like, the beginning part. Most women are like that. We need time to warm up. Why is this hard for you guys to understand? You're the first people to tell us not to gun a cold engine. You want us to go from zero to sixty in a minute. We're not built like that. We stall.

—*Anita Wise*

You know why God is a man? Because if God was a woman she would have made sperm taste like chocolate.

—*Carrie Snow*

I love the lines
men use to get us into bed.
"Please, I'll only put it in
for a minute."
What am I,
a microwave?

—*Beverly Mickins*

—SEX EDUCATION—

Conservatives say teaching sex education in the public schools will promote promiscuity. With our education system? If we promote promiscuity the same way we promote math or science, they've got nothing to worry about.

—*Beverly Mickins*

I was very sheltered growing up. I knew nothing about sex. My mother said this: "Sex is a dirty, disgusting thing you save for somebody you love."

—*Carol Henry*

—SHOPPING—

Shopping is better than sex. If you're not satisfied after shopping, you can make an exchange for something you really like.

—*Adrienne Gusoff*

I was street smart—but unfortunately the street was Rodeo Drive.

—*Carrie Fisher*

I am partial to the grocery store because it is one of the few places on earth where I can afford to buy pretty much any item I want. I never find myself seduced by a perfect melon, picturing my friends seething with jealousy when they get a gander at my newest acquisition, only to look at the tag and discover that it costs $159 and needs to be dry cleaned.

—*Sarah Dunn*

The only time a woman has a true orgasm is when she's shopping. Every other time she's faking it.

—*Joan Rivers*

*Buying something on sale
is a very special feeling. In fact,
the less I pay for something,
the more it is worth to me. I have
a dress that I paid so little for that
I am afraid to wear it.
I could spill something on it,
and then how would I replace it
for that amount of money?*

—Rita Rudner

I would rather have a sharp stick in my eye
than go shopping.
—*Kate Clinton*

—SLEEP—

Sleep is death without the responsibility.
—*Fran Lebowitz*

Can you remember when you didn't want to sleep? Isn't it inconceivable?
I guess the definition of adulthood is that you want to sleep.

—*Paula Poundstone*

—SMALL TOWNS—

It was such a small town we didn't have a village idiot. We had to take turns.

—*Billy Holliday*

SMOKING—

*To someone who commented that
she couldn't get to heaven with smoke on her breath:*
Yes, chile, but when I goes to heaven
I expect to leave my breath behind.

—*Sojourner Truth*

—SOLITUDE—

I'm single because I was born that way.

—*Mae West*

One of the advantages
of living alone
is that you don't have to
wake up in the arms
of a loved one.

—Marion Smith

We're all in this together—by ourselves.

—*Lily Tomlin*

—SPACE EXPLORATION—

I think the space program really needs to be
rethought. Our whole approach to space has
been very male. We went up to the moon.
We walked around on it. And we never came
back. We never called. We never wrote.
It's the typical one-night stand.

—*Beth Lapides*

Golf is not a sport.
Golf is men in ugly pants, walking.

—*Rosie O'Donnell*

About football: You might just as well put
in your time watching a lot of ants running
in and out of their hole.

—*Lorena Hickok*

Give a man a fish and you feed him for a day. Teach a man to fish, and you get rid of him on weekends.

—*Nancy Gray*

Every time a baseball player grabs his crotch, it makes him spit. That's why you should never date a baseball player.

—*Marsha Warfield*

Whoever said,
"It's not whether you
win or lose that counts,"
probably lost.

—*Martina Navratilova*

Baseball is what we were,
football is what we have become.
—*Mary McGrory*

Those football players aren't so hot...
take away the helmets, the shoulder pads,
the jerseys, the tight pants—
and what do you have? Oh my gosh!
—*Marie Mott*

My mom said she learned how to swim.
Someone took her out in the lake and threw her
off the boat and that's how she learned how
to swim. I said, "Mom, they weren't trying
to teach you how to swim."

—*Paula Poundstone*

—STRESS—

I read this article. It said the typical symptoms
of stress are eating too much, smoking too
much, impulse buying, and driving too fast. Are
they kidding? This is my idea of a great day!

—*Monica Piper*

—SUCCESS—

There is no point at which you can say,
"Well, I'm successful now.
I might as well take a nap."

—*Carrie Fisher*

—TELECOMMUNICATIONS—

At the end of every year, I add up the time
that I've spent on the phone on hold
and subtract it from my age.
I don't count that time as really living.

—*Rita Rudner*

It says a lot about your life what you have on your speed dial. I have two things on mine and I get them confused: the take-out chicken place and the suicide hotline. You don't know what it's like to be bawling your eyes out for twenty minutes and some lady breaks in, "You want the nine-piece bucket or the twelve-piece bucket?" I don't know how many times I've called the suicide hotline to see what's holding my chicken up.

—Joan Keiter

For a list of all the ways technology has
failed to improve the quality of life,
please press three...
—*Alice Kahn*

Many are called but few are called back.
—*Mary Tricky*

We don't care. We don't have to.
We're the phone company.

—*Lily Tomlin, as Ernestine*

Book title: Hi. This is Sylvia. I can't come
to the phone right now, so when you hear
the beep, please hang up.

—*Nicole Hollander*

—TELEVISION—

The whole world isn't watching anymore—
it's renting videos.
—*Julia Willis*

Television has proved that people will look
at anything rather than each other.
—*Ann Landers*

*I'm at a point where
I want a man in my life—
but not in my house!
Just come in,
attach the VCR,
and get out.*

—Joy Behar

I eat too many TV dinners. I've gotten to the point where every time I see aluminum foil I start to salivate.

—*Ellen Orchid*

About criticizing a television show in development:
Why would even a critic criticize something that doesn't exist? It's like seeing a sonogram and saying the baby's ugly.

—*Paula Poundstone*

My children refused to eat anything
that hadn't danced on TV.

—*Erma Bombeck*

—THANKSGIVING—

I have strong doubts that the first Thanksgiving
even remotely resembled the "history" I was told in
second grade. But considering that (when it comes
to holidays) mainstream America's traditions tend
to be overeating, shopping, or getting drunk,
I suppose it's a miracle that the concept of giving
thanks even surfaces at all.

—*Ellen Orleans*

—THERAPY—

I've been trying to find ways to overcome my inferiority complex. I considered therapy, till I saw the listings in the yellow pages: "Abusive Relationships," "Eating Disorders," "Drug Addiction." I only have low self esteem. My problems aren't good enough.

—*Anita Wise*

I went to a conference for bulimics and anorexics....The bulimics ate the anorexics.

—*Monica Piper*

The problem with therapy
is it takes me
more than fifty minutes
to calm down enough
to get in touch with
my anxiety.

—Lori Sprecher

—TIME—

The future isn't what it used to be.
—*Linda Moakes*

I've been on a calendar but never on time.
—*Marilyn Monroe*

—TRAVEL—

Is there anything as horrible as starting on a trip? Once you're off, that's all right, but the last moments are earthquake and convulsion, and the feeling that you are a snail being pulled off your rock.

—Anne Morrow Lindbergh

To put it rather bluntly, I am not the type who wants to go back to the land; I am the type who wants to go back to the hotel.

—Fran Lebowitz

You ever hear of Freud airlines?
They have two sections.
Guilt and non-guilt.
The seats go all the way back...to childhood.
—*Ellen Orchid*

I don't mind hecklers.
I know how to ignore people.
I was an airline stewardess.

—*Joanne Dearing*

The bus scares me.
Sixty-five people on the bus
and I was the last one on.
I felt like calling
<u>Unsolved Mysteries.</u>
"Yeah, I found everybody."

—Kathleen Madigan

—TRUTH—

I never know how much of what I say is true.
—*Bette Midler*

—TWINS—

We were born ten minutes apart,
Adrian first. She always said she was
the real baby, and I was a kind of backup.
—*Adair Lara*

—UNDERWEAR—

What is Victoria's Secret?
My guess is that she likes to dress like a slut.
—*Carol Siskind*

Brevity is the soul of lingerie.
—*Dorothy Parker*

My Playtex Living Bra died—
of starvation.

—*Phyllis Diller*

I'll tell you what Victoria's Secret is.
The secret is that nobody that's thirty-four
inches or thirty-four years
can fit into that shit.

—*Mary Ann Nichols*

*Like every good
little feminist-in-training
in the sixties, I burned
my bra—and now it's the
nineties and I realize Playtex
has supported me better than
any man I've ever known.*

—Susan Sweetzer

A lady is one who never
shows her underwear intentionally.

—*Lillian Day*

—**WAR**—

You can no more win a war than
you can win an earthquake.

—*Jeanette Rankin*

I have just come up with
a wonderful solution to end all wars—
let men give directions on how to get there.

—*Erma Bombeck*

If women ruled the world and we all
got massages, there would be no war.

—*Carrie Snow*

Non-violence is a flop.
The only bigger flop is violence.
—*Joan Baez*

—WEATHER—

I was really happy when they started naming
hurricanes after men. It made national
disasters sound even more like my
emotional life. "Brian Wrecks All" could be
a headline from my journal.

—*Regina Barreca*

—WOMEN—

"Slut" used to mean
a slovenly woman. Now it means
a woman who will go to bed
with everyone. This is considered
a bad thing in a woman, although
perfectly fabulous in a man.
"Bitch" means a woman who will
go to bed with everyone but you.

—*Cynthia Heimel*

God made man, and then said
I can do better than that and made woman.

—Adela Rogers St. Johns

Any woman who has a great deal to offer
the world is in trouble. And if
she's a black woman, she's in deep trouble.

—Hazel Scott

We haven't come a long way, we've come a short way. If we hadn't come a short way, no one would be calling us baby.

—*Elizabeth Janeway*

Calling women the weaker sex makes about as much sense as calling men the stronger one.

—*Gladiola Montana*

A woman without a man
is like fish without a bicycle.

—*Gloria Steinem*

The only problem with women
is men.

—*Kathie Sarachild*

*Real equality is going to come
not when a female Einstein
is recognized as quickly as
a male Einstein, but when
a female schlemiel is promoted
as quickly as a male schlemiel.*

—Bella Abzug

To celebrate
"Take Your Daughter To Work Day" this year
we're both cleaning out the toilet.

—*Helene Siskind Parsons*

The hours are rough in advertising—
and in particular here at The Miller Agency.
Mike Miller has a saying:
if you don't come in on Saturday,
don't bother coming in on Sunday.

—*Karen Salmansohn*

There are very few jobs
that actually require a penis or vagina.
All other jobs should be open to everybody.

—*Flo Kennedy*

Adults are always asking little kids what
they want to be when they grow up
because they're looking for ideas.

—*Paula Poundstone*

I think of my boss as a father figure.
That really irritates her.

—*Mary Jo Crowley*

Whatever women must do
they must do twice as well as men
to be thought half as good.
Luckily, this is not difficult.

—*Charlotte Whitton*

About The Editor

Roz Warren is the editor of fifteen
collections of women's humor, including
the classic *Women's Glib*. She reviews humor
books and CDs for numerous publications,
and is working on her first novel.
She lives in Bala Cynwyd, Pennsylvania.